YOU
INSPIRE ME

GENE JOHNSTON

Gotham Books
30 N Gould St.
Ste. 20820, Sheridan, WY 82801
https://gothambooksinc.com/
Phone: 1 (307) 464-7800

© 2023 Gene R. Johnston. All rights reserved.
No part of this book may be reproduced, stored in a retrieval system, or transmitted by any means without the written permission of the author.

Published by Gotham Books (March 23, 2023)

ISBN: 979-8-88775-225-9   H
ISBN: 979-8-88775-223-5   P
ISBN: 979-8-88775-224-2   E

Any people depicted in stock imagery provided by iStock are models, and such images are being used for illustrative purposes only.

Certain stock imagery © iStock.

Because of the dynamic nature of the Internet, any web addresses, or links contained in this book may have changed since publication and may no longer be valid. The views expressed in this work are solely those of the author and do not necessarily reflect the views of the publisher, and the publisher hereby disclaims any responsibility for them.

INTRODUCTION

These pages contain the inner thoughts and prayers of Gene Johnston who has truly been transformed into God's MUDD. By letting Him shape and mold his life as God sees fit, he has come to see life with different eyes, and understanding.

You Inspire Me is a powerful collection seeking to permeate feelings of love, hope, and peace throughout the reader. While most of the poetry is written in prose, this unique free writing format clearly gives the text rhythm, structure, and unity that would be nonexistent if the poems were individualized. Unlike your typical run-of-the-mill poems, Gene's poetry has an identity, a voice that resonates with meaning. His words are brimming with conviction as they pleadingly guarantee a shift in the way one sees life.

DEDICATION

I dedicate this book to my family. Because without the love, support, encouragement, and the inspiration that came from my family half of the things, I have ever accomplished in my life would not have been possible.

I also dedicate this book to all those who feel lost, lonely, and unloved. I pray that with these poems will help you realize that you can achieve any dream or goal that you may have, and that any disability, person, or setback can't stand in your way.

TABLE OF CONTENTS

INTRODUCTION

DEDICATION

YOU INSPIRE ME
A NEW DAY
DOUBTING HEART
BRIGHTER DAYS
FADING AWAY
HEAVENLY EYES
HAY YOU

HOLD ON TO ME
I FOUND LOVE IN YOU
I HAVE LOVE TO GIVE
I KNOW
IF I THOUGHT
LOVE TRANSFORMED
LOVING FATHER
MY LOVE
NEVER STOP
"OH, MY ANGEL"
OPEN YOUR HEART

REMEMBER WHEN
RESTLESS SOUL
SHADOWS OF THE NIGHT
SLEEP, MY LOVE
STARSHINE
SUNRISE: SUNSET
SUNRISE
"OH, SWEETHEART"
THANK YOU

THE BOND
THAT HUMAN HEART
THE STROLL
TO LOVE ME
UNIVERSAL TIES
WALK ON
WALKING BLIND
WE ARE ONE:
WEARY TRAVELER
WHAT IS THIS

WHAT SHOULD I DO
WITHOUT YOU
YOU LIFT ME UP
A LEAF ON THE OCEAN
A BRAND-NEW DAY
THE BATTLE
COME TO ME
DON'T YOU KNOW
DREAMS
DREAMS OF YOU

YOU INSPIRE ME

You inspired me just by looking into my eyes

The radiance of your beautiful face lights up any room you are in

Your words lift the brokenhearted. The love you have for others changes lives forever;

So good to you because your Inspiration brings out the best in me

Your inspiration encourages me to try my best and to be good to you all the time

Even when I don't share your views,

you will not judge me

When I keep my distance, and I keep my secrets,

you will not push me

When I can't tell you why you still do not judge me

You just accept me for who I am.

And even through it all, you may see me struggling

But with your words, and your love you will never let me fail.

Yes, you are that thorn in my flesh, you have this way

about you that digs in deep into my very soul,

and sees me for who

I've become, and help me grow as a better" person

I'm happy to bear this thorn in my flesh for without it my

life would be unfulfilled.....

A NEW DAY

A new day has come with new challenges and

New horizons

Have you seen to it that you're ready for the

"Responsibilities and the task that lies before you?"

Have you seen to it that your

mentally, physically, spiritually ready?

Come walk with me so that we can share all that has

been prepared for us this day

Come talk with me so that our minds will be

at peace with all

Life is not about the past. Life is not about the future

Life is not about the present

Life is about seeking God!

So always seek what is right and Noble,

and live each day as if it's your last

So have a wonderful day!

DOUBTING HEART

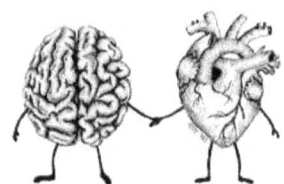

I just gotta know that your love is true because all my love

is waiting just for you

If I let you come inside my heart; will you be there for

me when I need someone to hold

Baby don't misunderstand me I just need a little time

before I invest my love in you

You said all the things that I like to hear

you pushed all

My buttons, and I want to feel your love for me for sure

I need to know that you need me, every night

"I pray that tomorrow never comes, so that I can keep"

you all to myself always and forever.....

BRIGHTER DAYS

Right from the start, it's been your burning love

And your healing love that has saved me from a world of loneliness

Oh, baby can't you see that it's been written in the

Stars, and in the scars on our hearts that we were

always meant to be?

Oh, baby now that I found you; there are going to be

brighter days before for us. Because I will never say that I've had enough of

your love

I will take you in my arms, and hold you right where you

belong 'till the day my life is through.

FADING AWAY

Sometimes I feel as if I'm fading away

I see all my life in front of me and ask myself "What have I accomplished?"

I often hear defeat and regret whispering into my ear

Failure and misery often follow

But only when despair and anguish come into my life do you come and lift me with your words

"You are much more caring, loving, kind and romantic than you can ever think of"

"So Do not fear, for I am with you; do not be dismayed,

for I am your God"

"Know that I am always with you and will

Never forsake you"

"I can always say even at my worst, you love me"

You wrap your arms around me, and you hold me close

Even at my worst, you give me something that I don't deserve

Your love!

When you lift me, I am no longer fading into the

Background, I no longer wish to hide, for you are always with me

"You will always love me!"

HEAVENLY EYES

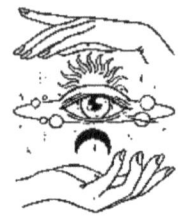

I'm telling you to look at life through heavenly eyes

Not human eyes

Know that you were not abandoned in all your wandering

You were not left alone in your darkest times

And know that this is where you realize that the Father has great designs for you,

And his love will be the tie that binds us together

All the stars have all aligned this day, and right now is

The perfect time to say; "I Love You"

Every sunrise gives us a new beginning and a new ending Let this morning be a new beginning to a better relationship; let it be an ending to the bad memories

Let us make it an

Opportunity to enjoy life, breathe freely, think and love

It is time that we leave behind our past

And know that through it all the hardest part was letting go of ourselves

Know that there is a greater love that holds us in his hands..

HAY YOU

Hay you, you tell me there's no hope at all

But I keep moving upward and onward, for nothing is going to keep me down

Hay you, out there in the darkness; are you getting tired

of being cold, lonely, and getting old?

Can you hear my cry echoing in the darkness pleading for you to come to me?

Hay you, don't give in without a fight, and don't help

them to bury the light

Hay you, I'm so tired and worn out from carrying this

burden that's on my back

Would you help me to carry it and give me some rest?

Hay you, there's a time that I remember, when I did not

know any pain

When I believed in forever, everything would stay the same

Hay you, there's a time that I remember when

I never felt so lost

When I felt all of the hatred was too powerful to stop

Hay you, now my heart feels like an ember and it's

lighting up the dark.

And I'll carry these torches for you and you know I will never drop them.

HOLD ON TO ME

As I stand in the dark and all alone. All I ask of you is that

you hold on to me!

I find that when you are not near to me or that

I have gone far from your side that my

heart yearns for your presence

So let your arms wrap around me as if they are a blanket

and cover me with your love, mercy, and kindness

I pray that you hold on to me as if there is no tomorrow.

"Chasing all the darkness, loneliness, and fears away."

I FOUND LOVE IN YOU

Know that every moment that you smile it chases all of

my pain, and darkness away.

I have never felt that I could be all that you wanted.

From the first moment, we met It was like our hearts

were intertwined in perfect harmony.

I have never been the same from the moment

your love for me came and filled my life.

When I felt your love for me, I almost didn't recognize it

because it happened very fast

And I wanted to make that moment last forever

You are forever in my heart and this is where you'll

always stay

For reasons I cannot explain my life has become better

But when we are apart you keep me company even in my dreams

So, for you, I leave this persisting message;

Even in the darkest night,

the light of your love shows me the way

And this is the reason why I love you

I HAVE LOVE TO GIVE

I have love to nurture you

I have love to give you

I'm at the door of your heart that overflows

With powerful emotions

My heart believes in you

I'm getting ready to make you my woman for life

I'll be there to comfort you

I'll be there to celebrate with you

I'll rejoice when you do and pacify you when you're down

My love will kick the pain of hurt far from your heart

You're the right one for me

I won't blow your mind away with empty promises, but

with love and actions that'll never leave a doubt,

but fill your heart with joy

I'm here to give you the best miracle you've ever

experienced and that's "LOVE."

I KNOW

What I know is that your future will be fulfilled through
your courage
And though my eyes have never seen you
I've seen enough to say I know that You are good, kind and
that you are so much more than meets the eye
I know that you have been the calm within the storm
that has been raging in my life
 I know that sometimes this weight is overwhelming to me
but thank God, I don't have to carry it alone because of you
You have seen my darkest days and shared some of
my deepest pain
Through it all, you have listened and cared for me
I know I can't begin to describe the connection I feel
with you, I only know it's there and I miss it when I don't talk to you.
I know I smile more than I did before, I know I feel less
alone than I did before,
I know I feel the purpose in my life where there was none
before, and I know that I am not alone anymore.

IF I THOUGHT

If I thought for just one moment

that this would be my last breath

I'd tell you that I'll love you forever,

and even beyond death

If I thought for just one moment

that your face would be the last thing I'd see;

I'd take a million pictures and save them just for me

If I thought for just one moment that your voice

would be the last thing I'd hear, I'd listen attentively and

promise not to shed one tear

If I thought for just one moment that your touch would

be the last thing that I'd feel,

I'd embrace you and know that this has all been real

If I thought just for one moment that my heart would

beat it's the last beat today

I'd thank the Lord for allowing us to meet.

LOST WITHOUT YOU

"Well, another day has gone by without you and I find
myself thinking of all the wonderful times we had together
So, I sit here silently crying
because the path I am on is without you
I have always found that you fulfilled my deepest dreams
I never want to meet the person I was ever again
Because I hid behind a brick wall and woke up tired and
broken from the all mistakes, I had made the day before
The day we met was the happiest day of my life
Because not only did you lift me out of the lifeless feeling
of loneliness, dread, and misery,
but you gave me hope for the first time in my life
You showed me the true meaning of love, kindness,
and compassion just by being there for me
When I wander from your side
I have found that
I'm lost without you in my life....

LOVE TRANSFORMED

Ever since I have found you my life

has become a better place

Oh, my how my life without you was sadder

and a darker place

The day we met you transformed my life into something

Indescribable;

You made me see things that I could not have seen before

Oh, my love know that you are the air I breathe,

and know that if I told you once I told you a thousand times

that I'll never leave you

Hold on to me and I will transfer all my joy,

and warmth to you

As I have transferred it to all those that have cross my path.

LOVING FATHER

Hello my child,

I have left this letter for you to be read on the day you decided to leave my home

First of all, I want you to know that you were always loved, and wanted even before you were conceived.

I know that I was not always physically there for you, but know that you were in my heart

I know you may have felt alone, and abandoned at times, but know that you never were alone because I cried when you cried

I hurt when you hurt, I rejoiced when you rejoiced and I prayed when you prayed

I have done everything in my power to prepare you for this journey you must now take;

Up to this point in your life, I have made sure that you have never gone without

I want you to take comfort in the thought that there was never a time that I did not love you
No matter how mad you got at me or what you may have said to me or about me
My love for you only grew.
Even in the times when you cursed my name
And told me that you hated me; my love for you could not be dismissed...

There has been no greater honor bestowed upon me to witness you becoming into your own.
I want you to know that no matter where your journey takes you; you will never find a purer, truer, unconditional love than I have for you.

MY LOVE

My love, I had a dream that you were with me, and you we're holding my heart in your hands

My love, know that you mean so much to me and that I will never forget the impact you had on my life

My love, know that this is where I want you to be forever

My love, know that I'm in your arms,

And I feel your love towards me

I know deep down you will never hurt me

My love, I want you to know if you truly love me, and be with me and get to know who I am?

My love, know that all my love is yours forever and that I think of you all the time.

NEVER STOP

If I have learned one thing in life,
and that one thing would be that choosing you to complete my life has
empowered me to become the person
I am today.

With your guiding principles of love, hope, and
forgiveness I have built a fortress that can withstand any test of time that
might give it.

With you beside me, we are one step closer to becoming more than we can
ever dream to become,
and doing the impossible as one.

I can ask of you is to never stop believing in the fact
that together we are stronger,
And nothing can put an end to what God has started.

"OH, MY ANGEL"

Good night my Angel, it's time to close your
eyes and sleep
Oh, my Angel, I often wonder if you can feel the love I
have for you while you sleep

Oh, my Angel, I find it hard to let you sleep because I
know that holding on to someone when their gone is harder
than letting them go when they are with you
Sleep tight my Angel because when I close my eyes I
see you here with me
Know this my Angel that there is nothing you can't
accomplish when you have love in your heart, a smile on
your face, and the courage to dream

Oh God, I think I'm falling out of the sky, Heaven helps
me it's like a dream
Oh, my Angel you were like a thief because you stole

my heart and I was your willing victim

Oh, my angel I let you see the parts of me, that was not all that pretty, and with every touch, you fixed them...

OPEN YOUR HEART

All I ask of you is for you to open your heart to me, and
let me show you the love I have for you
If I promise you that I will never run away from you;
Will you open your heart to me, baby?
Oh, baby, I think that you're afraid to look in my eyes
because you have forgotten how to love, and you have
chosen to look the other way.

Well, I've got something to say to you...I hold the lock
and you hold the key that opens your heart to me, darlin',
and I'll give you all my love if you only turn the key for me

This I promise you; I've loved you forever and In
lifetimes before
I promise you that you will never feel lonely anymore.
I give you my word and with this vow to you;
My heart is yours forever and that this is a
battle we have won
We are one for now and forever...

REMEMBER WHEN

When I hear of your endless love and mercy,

And I see the power of your written Word that changes

men's lives forever I can say that I am truly blessed

Because I remember when you were there with every beat

of my heart

Because I remember when you were there in every breath I

took

Because I remember when you were there in every

sunrise I saw

Because I remember when you were there when I was

on my knees talking to you.

RESTLESS SOUL

I need you to lead me home with your strong hands,
because I'm just a restless soul, and I know that I can't do it
alone

Oh, hold on to me and let me live in your
loving arms forever
Hold me tight and drive that restless soul
far from me

Your love for me has driven that restless soul from my
heart and has become my guiding light
Your love for me also has helped me discover that life can
be rich and beautiful
I know with you in my life I will never lack for anything
ever again

Your love for me has awakened a new person, and a part of
me that I thought was long dead
Your love for me has made me realize that there is

more to life than an endless journey into the darkness

Your love for me has made me want to show it to the

world so that others may know of its beauty.

SHADOWS OF THE NIGHT

Oh, baby take my hand, and surrender all your dreams
to me, and know that everything will be alright
Come and give your heart to me baby so that I can take
all the pain that you have ever felt go away
Let me tell you how good it feels to be with you this
night
Holding you while the shadows of the night play outside
our window
What we are experiencing is something unpredictable and
know that in the end, it's right
So, know this, all we ever need is each other and nobody
else, so don't ever think of giving up, just take a moment to
decide what you want out of life
because it is worthwhile
I know that you have waited so long for this moment in
your life
Be strong for me baby, and hold your head high because we
will always have each other.

SLEEP, MY LOVE

Go to sleep my Love, my Angel, my all

Go and chase your dreams while you lay in my arms

tonight

I only ask that for just this moment in time so that you

can be all mine

You have a long road before you so rest your weary

head, and when you arise in the morning think of what

a precious privilege it is to be alive, to breathe, to think, to

enjoy, to love

So, take photographs in your mind of this moment;

For it may be the last one we have on this Earth

Sleep my love my Angel, my all, and be comforted to

know that you are wrapped in my loving arms.

STARSHINE

Oh, Starshine you are that small light in the distant sky.

You stand alone out in the darkness shining ever so

bright.

Oh, Starshine you say; "You feel so alone, and afraid."

Come to me so that we can diminish that feeling together.

Oh, Starshine I stand out in the rain and I can see your

pain and hear your heart, come to me drive out the darkness in

my life

Oh, Starshine some face a lifetime of pain and

suffering

Well, I've had my share of troubles and suffering, but

compared to yours mine are only days or years.

Oh, Starshine come light up my life so that we shall

never walk alone again. Shine upon me your rays of hope

and drive out all those bad feelings

Oh, Starshine come to me so that we can walk

together, and lift each other for the long journey before us.

SUNRISE: SUNSET

Each morning I wake up to once again to witness your

power, love, and greatness

You show me just in the sunrise of your power

Throughout the day you continue to show me your love

May it be a stormy day with no sunshine, you still show me

the power of your hand

As you guide me throughout the day, I see you hold

everything together with just your will

I can hear your voice in the quietness of my heart

Even if it seems like everything is against me and all

my hope seems to have vanished;

I can find strength in your love

Then as the day comes to an end you remind me once

again, just who is in charge of the beauty of the sunset and

with the coming stars, you show it all to me again.

SUNRISE

As the sun rises in the East, it's not just a reminder of a new day
The sunrise is a symbol of love, kindness, and strength, but most of all it's a reminder that all is okay!

My words fail to describe what I see before me
As my words fail to describe how I feel about you
Yes, I could say "I Love You"
but what I feel about you goes way beyond those three words
Like the sunrise, it inspires me with new life, but you inspire me to be better

When I hear or read the words from your heart it sets me on fire
And most of all just you being there for me tells me all is okay!

So, know this as the sun knows to rise in the East

That you are loved, you are cherished, but most of all you

have someone here for you

So as the sunrise worms the day, and brings light to all

who lives this day

I say these words to you; I love you, I cherish you, I

worship you, but most of all know that you are mine to hold.

"OH, SWEETHEART"

Oh, Sweetheart; Let me light that fire within your soul.

Oh, Sweetheart; I have a river of love to give to you.

Oh, Sweetheart; I place myself in your arms to have and to hold forever.

Oh, Sweetheart I ask that you just hold me tight and never let me go.

Oh, Sweetheart; I'm drowning in this ocean of love because of you.

Oh, Sweetheart; Please don't rescue me, because I'm okay this way.

Oh Sweetheart: I am never letting you go so another person to steal you away from me!

THANK YOU

I wake up in the morning to see your face in sleep, and
say a quick prayer,
"Thank you, Lord, for blessing me with this"
As I get up and look out the window I can't but stop and
admire the beauty and say again
"Thank you, Lord, for blessing me with this"
As I sit down for my morning devotional I once again
say,
"Thank you, Lord, for blessing me with this"

As my day goes on, I see hardship, hatred, love, temptation,
pain, beauty, greed, and all that man has to offer, I still say
"Thank you Lord for blessing me with this"
As a ready myself for bed and look over into your eyes
And say, "Thank you Lord for blessing me with this.
Thank you for the blessings I cannot begin to count,
Thank you for the beauty and the Ugliness in this world.
Thank you for my family.
 Thank you for the trials and temptations.

Thank you for giving me what I need and no more.

Thank you for your hardship and wealth.

Most of all Thank you for being You."

THE BOND

Why do you test me like this? why do you say words
that set my heart on fire?
What do you see in my soul that no one else sees?
Do You think you can come into my life and turn it upside
down?
What have I ever done to you to merit your time, your love,
your respect, your devotion, your beauty, or even your
laughter?
If this is how I am to be treated after I have opened my
arms, my heart, and my very soul to you
Well, all I can say is <u>"Thank You!"</u>
It is because of these facts that I can now promise that
our lives will never be the same.
I don't understand this bond that we now share, because it
goes beyond simple words like love, relationship, and
marriage.
Because we are now bounded in this way we now
share Intimacy the way God intended it to be.
From your lover, your soulmate, your husband, your
one and all

THAT HUMAN HEART

From the first time we met, I discovered that what we
have now is no ordinary love.
When love came to me, it caught me off-guard.
It was so easy to miss it and not notice that it was alive
within me.

It's a funny thing that the human heart feels and how it can
overlook; and overcome things like the loneliness in your
eyes, the need for someone to cry with, or the passion for
life itself.

We tend to not see the love and cranny of others' lives.
Carrying us to new heights and awareness than we have
ever known before.
I can't believe the peace; I'm feeling right now
knowing that there is a special place within my
heart just for you.

THE STROLL

As we stroll along the pathway set before us,

I can see the love dancing in your eyes.

The dancing light in your eyes reminds me of little fireflies.

Oh, how the joy of seeing you like this makes my heart fuller.

Oh, what joy you bring into my life, and knowing that you are so happy has fulfilled my wildest dreams.

While strolling with you this evening I think back on all the times we have shared. Oh, how I want to dance with you as the light dances in your eyes.

As we stroll along, we cling to each other as if we are one.

Not saying one word because we are afraid that any sound

might break this magical moment.

The words "*I LOVE YOU*" cannot begin to describe what I

feel at this moment. So, I hold you even tighter praying to

God almighty for this night will never end.

TO LOVE ME

(A Woman's View)

To love me is, When I feel alone, empty, and a

stranger, I know you are there for me.

When your eyes tell me I am the person you love, and that

you want me for who I am.

To love me; is when you never abandon me when in

my darkest hour.

To know that I don't need you to coddle me like a child, I

need you to treat me with respect and kindness for the person I

am.

To love me; is, to show me through verbal, visual,

emotional, spiritual, and physical cues.

To put down what you reading, to turn off the TV, to stop

what you are doing and listen to me,

To love me; is, to know when to shut up and hold your tongue, when you know that I need comforting words, or to just be held tight.

To love me; is when you see behind the mask I wear
and accept me as I am and who I have become.
To see all the little imperfections I have,
and still say "I love you!"

UNIVERSAL TIES

"Come," said the Muse, to me and sing a song that no one has yet written.
Put into words all your feelings, and bind us in that universal language of love, hope, peace, and harmony.

You're the only part of me
I'm certain that will live on.

We have universal ties that can only be understood by God.
I for one never believed that anything could feel this
true.

So come and lay your weary head down on my shoulder
and don't cry anymore.

WALK ON

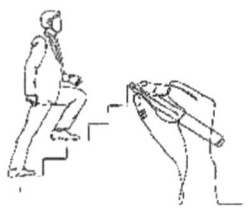

When you walk through a storm;

Hold your head up high.

And don't be afraid of the dark.

At the end of the storm

Is a golden sky

And the sweet silver song of a lark.

Walk on through the wind.

Walk on through the rain.

Though' your dreams are tossed and blown.

Walk on, walk on

With hope in your heart

And you'll never walk alone no; you'll never walk alone

WALKING BLIND

I was walking like a dead man, and you rescued me

from the darkness; you have chased that part of me that

loves to play in the shadows in the night away.

With your love, you rescued me from me.

You had no judgment, malice, or hatred within you;

only love, mercy, and understanding.

Before you came into my life I was living in a world of

death. But your love made me see how to be truly free

Before you; I had no fear of the night; because we were

one.

Oh, how I loved walking in the dark; because I thought I

could hide and play all the time.

Through your love for me, you have shown me a world

of happiness, beauty, and wonders.

I truly have been blessed to have someone like you to love

me!

WE ARE ONE

"The human language is spoken in several languages,"

but only one voice.

"The language is not English, Spanish, Italian, or"

"Chinese, nor is it, German."

It speaks in the language of hope.

It speaks in the language of trust.

It speaks in the language of strength and the language

of compassion.

It is the language of the heart and the language of the

soul.

It is always one voice.

"It is the voice of our ancestors, speaking through us."

And the voice of our inheritors waiting to be born.

"It is that small, still voice in all of us saying."

We are one!

No matter the skin color.

No matter the nation.

We are one!

No matter the pain.

No matter the darkness.

No matter the loss.

No matter the fear.

We are one!

WEARY TRAVELER

Weary traveler, are you beat down from the storms that you have weathered?

Weary traveler, do you feel like this road just might go on forever?

Weary traveler Is your tired heart on the edge of breaking?

Be still oh restless soul know that you were never meant to walk this road alone

Weary traveler you need to know that someday it will be worth it all, so just hold on.

Weary traveler, you won't be weary long. No, you won't be weary long because someday soon we're gonna make it home.

Weary traveler, what road are you on?

WHAT IS THIS

What is this feeling that you have awakened from within me?

Oh, please tell me what it is!

What is this feeling of dread and yet of happiness I now feel?

Oh, please tell me what it is!

What is this feeling of hunger and want I now have every time I see you, hear your voice, or even read your words?

Oh, please tell me what it is?

Oh, how do you begin to describe this feeling I now have in one word?

This feeling of hunger, dread, happiness, want, excitement, wonder, pain, joy, and so many other feelings all wrapped up in one?

Oh, please tell me how it is possible for one person to feel so lost and alone for one second and then find themselves in a state that one can only describe as complete?

Could you tell me what this feeling is?

WHAT SHOULD I DO

Before I met you, I felt that I couldn't love anyone and that nobody would be able to fill the void in my heart; but that all changed when I met you......

Then I came to the realization you were always on my mind.

You're funny and sweet, you make me laugh and smile, you take away all my anger and sadness, and you are the most beautiful woman that I have ever seen; more beautiful than any flower ever to bloom.

You make me weak whenever I talk to you, and then I started to write poems about you.
Now I come to realize that I am hopelessly in love with you

WITHOUT YOU

Oh, my love, I found that when you are gone from my side I begin to miss the sight of you standing next to me.
Oh, how I miss the sound of your heartbeat in my ear.
Oh, how I miss the smell of you near me.

Oh, my love, I have found that if you are gone for too long I can still see you out of the corner of my eye.
And when I close my eyes, you appear right before me wearing that outfit that makes you so Irresistible.
And to make matters worse when I see that sparkle in your eye and that stupid smile on your face that tells me that you love me more than words can ever convey.

Oh, my love, I have found that my heart feels a little heavy when I don't hear from you for so long, and I have a hard time getting motivated.
Oh, please hurry back to my side, to where you belong.
Oh, my love, when you call me by my name my heart is

filled with so much love and compassion for you that I think I might die.

My love know this you were and always have been that answered prayer that I never prayed.

YOU LIFT ME UP

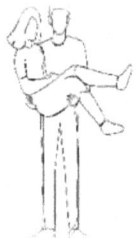

You lift me up, when I see the love you have for me, by all you do.
You lift me up, when I see how you provide for my loving family, or when I see the stars, you have made over my head.

You lift me up, when I am down, and I'm so weary and say "oh my soul."
You lift me up, when troubles come and my heart is burdened.

You lift me up, when all my insecurities take over me like a siren, and I can't hide them from you.
You lift me up, when I see my life as broken, and out of control.

And here in my silence you come and sit awhile with me. And it comforts me to know that there's no failure, no fall, or no sin you don't already know.

You knew I was so afraid that once you saw what was in me that you would turn your back on me and leave me in the silence, and darkness forever.

A LEAF ON THE OCEAN

I have set my course for the winds of the future.

I feel like I'm on a stormy sea of moving emotions.

Endlessly being tossed about like a ship on the ocean.

I have found that once I rise above this noise and confusion

of life, I can get a glimpse beyond here and now.

But I can hear the voices say to me

"It's a brand-new morning!

The day is a blank canvas yet to be painted with the colors

of life.

So, seize this day; because you may not have another!"

A BRAND-NEW DAY

The sun has risen over the crest of the Earth, and it's a start of a new day.

It's time to shake off the coils of sleep and embrace this new day with open arms.

Think of all the new adventures this day may bring to you.

Think of all of God's endless wonder's yet to be discovered.

Do not start this day with anger, hatred, or bitterness within your heart.

Instead, let the love I have for you fill you with joy and happiness.

THE BATTLE

We mount upon the wings of eagles and fly into the valley

of temptation,

and we commit our spirit into Your mighty hands.

Oh Lord God of truth you have ransomed us this day, and

You have armed us with the shield of faith and the sword of

the Spirit, then you have clothed us in righteousness.

In you, Oh Lord, we have taken refuge where we will never

be ashamed. Let us now open our mouths to make it known

that we are ready for battle.

You Oh Lord, you have strengthened us and have given us

the battle this day, you have made us ambassadors over the fallen.

And when the battle is won,

we will rejoice in your presence, because we have glorified

Your name this day

AWAITING YOU

Just as the sunrise awaits you in the morning,

I also stand waiting for you with open arms.

Start your day right, start your day in my waiting loving

arms where they will hold you tight and never let you go.

Come rest your head on my shoulder and give me all your

fears. Know that my arms are strong and can carry all your

 burdens.

I will wait for you to make your choice, so will you rush

into these open arms, or will you choose to stay in the

 darkness alone?

COME TO ME

I can hear you crying in the darkness.
As I sit here with an open heart and out stretched arms
waiting for you to come to me.

I have cast the love I have for you into that darkness as
a beacon to safely guide you to my side.

Once you are in my arms you will find that the love,
I have for you has consumed all your fears, and loneliness,
then replaced it with hope and love.

I'm calling you to "come to me" so that my love for you
can
fill that void in your heart.

Come to me and let me show you the power of my
transforming love.

DON'T YOU KNOW

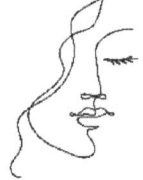

Don't you know; that when I hear you call my name it

makes my heart beat faster, and my soul soar?
Don't you know; that whenever I hear your voice it's like

an angel singing to me?

Don't you know; that If I didn't love you so much, life

would not be worth living?
Don't you know; that you can't play hide and seek with

your feeling for me?

Don't you know; that I know you feel that the love I have

for you is Undeserved?
Don't you know; that you are on your way to greater

things?

Don't you know; that there is no greater love than the love I

have for you?
Don't you know; that I am waiting with open arms for you

to come to me?

Don't you know; that I do all these things so that you may live?

Because if you don't know all this; you don't know me at all!

DREAMS

As I woke up from my lonely sleep,
I hoped more fervently even in my dreams to see the face

of my love again.
Your smile is what I'd rather behold than the brightness of

the sun from my window. Your promise of love is what

I'd hold onto stronger than the promise of life.
A breath shared with you is worth more than a lifetime of

gold without you.
Come what may on this day, I'll shower my love upon you

like the clouds of water upon the earth. Feel my love upon

the pleasure of your bed.
Express your love for me during the hurdles of the day.
In whatever I do today, your thoughts will be my muse as

they will in the years to come.
Be my love forever, be my love till eternity begins anew.

DREAMS OF YOU

As I woke up from a good night's rest with visions of you

still in my head;

Oh, how I prayed that this dream would never end!

Because I know that once I opened my eyes you would not

be there.

Oh, how I hold on to that dream as I lay there in my bed

knowing that I will hold fast to it.

And let it refresh, and strengthen me throughout the day.

Oh, my love I know you are not with me here in person but

be assured that you are in my heart.

Because I have witnessed your love for me first hand.

Even though you are not here in person I cherish every

memory of you and let it wash over me.

Living each moment of my day with happy thoughts and a

happy heart.

Do not Grieve for me my love, but take comfort in

the knowledge that we will be together in my dreams once

again this night.

www.ingramcontent.com/pod-product-compliance
Lightning Source LLC
LaVergne TN
LVHW061601070526
838199LV00077B/7130